TURNED TO LIGHT

SALMAN AKHTAR

Turned to Light

For Barbara
+ Leo
with much
admiration +
love

Salman

June '00

ADAMS PRESS
CHICAGO

Printed in the United States of America
Adams Press, Chicago

Library of Congress Catalog Card Number: 98-96921
ISBN: 0-9661852-4-2

Thanks to Maryann Nevin for skillful preparation of the manuscript and to Lauren Hansen-Flaschen for the photograph on the front cover. Two of the poems included here ("Conceptions" and "On the Body's Refusal to Sing") have appeared in the Fall 1998 issue of *Kala* (Toronto) and are published with it's editor's permission.

For

SAM GRAEBER
&
LYNN HANSEN-FLASCHEN

Childhood friends of Kabir and Nishat

CONTENTS

I

II

III

"Art is a wound turned to light."

(Georges Braque, 1934)

I

CONCEPTIONS

A big black cloud

dropped two smiling raindrops

in the purple courtyard

of the lotus on a satin lake.

A blue owl

and a pink mynah

flew out of the flower.

And the flower undulated with waves of lusty pride.

VIGIL

Not a word

has floated

across the river.

The old banyan tree,

Looks with sad expectation

at the white domes

Of the palace on the other

Bank.

QUESTIONS

What is the connection between weather and emotions?

Is generosity that seeks recognition still generosity?

Do trees talk to each other?

Why do fathers not write poems about their sons?

Can one succeed in failing?

Is food ever bad?

What makes a woman with a sore throat appear beautiful?

Why is water so accommodating?

Can one ever give more love than one has received?

How?

ANGUISH

(Edgartown, Mass. August 1996)

Broken glass is everywhere.

Feet bleed as I walk.

Opened skin reveals

unread manuscripts of pain.

The soothing drink of hitherto life,

spilled on the grey floor of decisions

The oblivion of hangover still too far.

A FATHER'S WISH

(for Nishat)

I pray, little girl

That your thirst does not lead you to empty wells.

That the clock on your mantle piece

        does not see friendless afternoons.

That fate does not deal you a cruel hand.

I pray.

But, my sweet, little darling, I also pray,

That when time comes

You will find within yourself

        the wit and courage

        to discard pouting princes

        in favor of

Playful paupers.

AT LAST

With aching legs,

tired eyes,

and the bourbon of hope

about to run out,

he came upon a turn.

Saw the house.

Tall, proud, and deep.

Beckoning him,

With promises of friendly gestures,

    familiar nicknames,

    hot meals and cool caresses.

RICH CONVERSATION

Silver laughter.

Ruby pauses.

Emerald hope,

    and then golden silence,

Till the next time

    on phone.

UPSTAIRS

("The best part of love is going upstairs" - Alberto Moravia)

Thousand strawberries.

Two melons.

Eight trees

One serpant.

and,

A lotus

appearing, disappearing, and reappearing

On a satin lake of breathless mutuality.

Is this crazy mathematics the product of a deranged mind?

Or, the private language of our love?

IT COMES IN WAVES

(Edgartown, Mass. August 1996)

Hope

a desperate, drowning animal

claws its way up the white verandah.

Sun

sips from a vast goblet of nostalgia.

Pain

and mocking guilt ride the frothy waves of ocean

Twenty feet away.

UNNAMED

A brief stay

In the house of dreams.

Thirty five lullabies of intricate plumbing.

Steel, blood, gauze, valium.

Euphemisms all.

Not one proper name,

before you left.

II

"The aesthetic moment constitutes a deep rapport between subject and object, and provides the person with a generative illusion of fitting with an object, evoking an existential memory. Existential, as opposed to cognitive, memory is conveyed not through visual or abstract thinking, but through the affects of being. Such moments feel familiar, uncanny, sacred, reverential, and outside cognitive coherence."

(Christopher Bollas, 1977)

ESSENCE

From the deep, brown cup of your body
through the silver lake of your mind,
to the diffuse ambience of your presence
somewhere in the house.
Then, from the diffuse ambience of your presence
somewhere in the house,
through the silver lake of your mind
to the deep, brown cup of your body
I travel again and again,
Back and forth.

And, in this journey
Lies the essence of my life.

ACROSS TIME

I hold

Your big little hand. Pull you

Across the chasm of history.

We come a bit closer.

But

The dye has been cast.

Your future is my past.

And, mine?

A darkness that, without you,

Will last and last.

RELENTLESS

Like truth.

Like a fabled, mad lover roaming the streets of the Orient.

Like the drum-roll of destiny.

Like a dark man driven to escape an unearned jail sentence.

Like fever.

Like Bombay's monsoon.

Like growing interest on money in the bank.

Like Rohan's questions, Tini's smiles.

Like time.

The smell of your unwashed breasts

follows me everywhere I go,

populates my each breath.

dances in my blood.

SO SHE SAID

Not content to be a mere raisin

in your life's bun,

I aspire to be a half-eaten chocolate

in your mouth.

Chewed, licked, crushed, rolled over.

Bathed in your manly saliva.

Finding specialness in the passing moments of our life.

Mourning

the irretrievable nature of each such moment.

THE MORNING PRAYER

In the liquid valley of unseen organs

little white fish swim proudly.

The lotus of extended limbs

welcomes the rising sun.

In the adjoining room

children open their sleepy eyes.

The day, my love, has begun.

SHARED PAIN

Anguish.

Be it on this side of the river

        or that,

        will always be our mutual property.

That is,

        till we live in the same house of love.

And this

I hope will be true

forever.

BEAR ME

Come. Have no fear.

Travel. Take me with you.

And, as you walk

Bear me like the sweet memory of your deceased uncle.

Bear me like the weight of your husband's prestige.

Bear me, in the psychic womb of your reverie,

    like the son you never had, never will.

    But more so,

Bear me like a cross

Of desperate, cavernous longing,

And, wistful loss!

EVIDENCES

A sudden stillness of the heart.

A bland coldness of the extremities,

A furtive pain around the mouth,

A desperate anguish in the eyes.

These are the evidences of your being distant from me.

SWEETHEART

Proximity with you

sets me aflame with desire.

Distance

sends me on the merry path of anticipation.

Holding you

is the paradise of soma.

Thinking about you,

is the heaven of mind.

Sweetheart

With your divine name on my lips,

I am dancing wildly

in this erotic delirium!

SIESTA MEMORY

Feet conspire.

Torsos get intertwined.

Unpainted fingernails play the soul's drum.

Intoxicated,

        the alphabet of the self

Gets scrambled.

Rearranged.

A GOOD MAP

Who could have thought

that the Lake of Forgiveness

will be in the Valley of Concern

not far from the Garden of Eroticism

and the Tower of intellect?

Who could have thought

that you will love me so much

and reverse all my misfortunes forever?

TOWARDS THE OCEAN

Undulating waves of desire, longing,

travel from one bank to the other.

Love's water washes the tired brow

of separation, waiting.

And the droplets of time

laugh like children,

as life's river flows

Towards the ocean of our endless togetherness.

CHOICELESS

In gleeful abandon,

With arms wide stretched, like a child

        pretending to be an airplaine,

With songs on lips,

With flutter in the heart,

        and butter under my feet,

I dash towards you.

Choiceless.

Madly in erotic passion.

Devoted in love.

ON THE BODY'S REFUSAL TO SING

The garden, my beloved, was yours.
All its mangos for your mouth alone,
        its red and yellow beaked parrots
        for you to behold, you to train.

Alas!
The scorching summer of disrespect
        has left all the trees fruitless, ashamed.
The birds either found home elsewhere,
        or, are too weak to flutter their wings.
This year, my darling,
The land is dry as a bone.

ONCE AGAIN

And

suddenly

the cactus of doubt,

grown in the soil of distance,

Withers.

Thoughtless memory

    speaks through muscles, blood,

    bones, wet surfaces.

As we travel towards

    each other

    for an embrace

Of erotic redemption.

REGARDLESS

Each night

Until you fall asleep,

I will stay awake.

Keep vigil.

I will be there when you wake up

Regradless

        of whom you dream of

        in your sleep.

MORNING WALK ON THE BEACH

The frothy symphony of the ocean

plays at our feet.

The sky still drunk from the night's black wine.

The impish wind steals my right to play

with you hair.

The silver of your briskly moving legs

melts with the warming up sun.

An unfamiliar liquid fills up the cup

of my heart.

With wonder and

Gratitude.

FREE-FALL

In a free-fall

of nature,

With no bungee of unfinished tasks

tying me to yesterday,

I gleefully descend from the roof of aloofness

to the courtyard

of our mutuality.

Leaving clouds, I became rain.

Fall

drop by drop!

THROUGHOUT THE FORTNIGHT

Beneath the patina of composure.

Besides the discipline of duty.

Between the drumbeats of industriousness.

Beyond the cacophony of admiration.

I kept in touch with you. Constantly.

heard your voice

felt the intoxicating sweep of your caress

smelled the scent of your body.

WATER

Like a cloud

I rise from your undulating blue generosity.

and

Like a raindrop

I return to your ever-forgiving bosom.

The journey between these two poles

of my existence

speaks of our inseparability.

III

RECIPE

(For Nishat, on her High School graduation)

Think hard, for hours, concentrate.
Then let go of the mind
Let the bird return to its nest
Let the mule rest.

Squeeze all the hatred out of your heart.
Wash the blood stains, clean the walls
Prepare the room for a loyal guest
Let intimacy be sacred, not a jest.

Walk, socialize, and sing. Dance and talk, become quiet.
Paint. Fall in love.
Stretch the limit. Take every test.
Let yourself contain both East and West.

To others, offer reparation; to self, love's healing potion
Slash the clouds, dig the earth, churn the ocean.
Go out in the world. Do your best.
Let my love accompany you in your every quest.

RETROSPECT

Flickering in my anguished eyes,

Written on my bleeding palms,

Transcribed on my ashen face,

        is the ugliness of a moment

        that came and went months ago.

Broke the mirror of my heart.

But its shards

        still reflect

The grace that existed before.

Trust, belonging, hope

        and more.

TO BREAK THE SPELL

Clawing its way through the skin of equanimity,

the inner hominid of pain emerges.

Mocking. Gleeful. Satan-like.

Wearing the crown of rage.

Breaking the momentary trance

of its evil glance,

I look for the sword of truth

to begin our last, bloody, and fatal dance!

A BAD ARGUMENT

The melody of mutual regard is torn.

Despair is thick.

Unspeakable emotions loom.

And, the smell of hatred

finds its way

To all the four nostrils in the room.

DILEMMA

(For Kabir)

Words

clumsy, fail.

Deeds

hollow praxis.

Thoughts

private, locked in mental trunk.

Feelings

liquid, raise anxiety, spill.

How then to convey

My pride in you

To you?

AREA CODE 307

Late last night

I came across

        the line of acceptance

        in the palm of your voice.

Reassured,

I put the receiver down

Slid into the sweet

Darkness of dreamless sleep.

THE REMEDY

(For Faiz Ahmad Faiz, of course)

Were music the ointment
    that soothed your soul,
I would play the flute, like Krishna.
Turn myself into a humble harp
Vibrate with each breath you take.

If words could ease your suffering some
I would spin yarns of utmost wonder, Like Schehrzade. Tales
    of wit and grace,
    of palaces and palanquins
    of beauty and bravery
    of sacrifice and wisdom
    of mango trees and shining nose rings
    of the deepest secrets held in the palms of lovers.

But the remedy of your pain, my friend,
    is nothing short of an amputation.
And, the hand that holds the scalpel,
    I tremble to tell you
    is but yours.

FIFTY TWO

Children leave home.

Area codes change.

Relationships dissolve.

Bridges break.

Lakes evaporate.

Uncles die.

Each moment the clock ticks.

This year I turn fifty two!

WARNING TO CIVILIANS

Beware of the man who feels at home on airports.

Beware of the woman who is dressed elegantly on Sunday mornings.

Beware of the man who never gives a gift to his nephew.

Beware of the woman who worries too much about her breasts.

Beware of the man who has slept with two women in the same day.

Beware of the woman who hates her father and has no son.

Beware, above all, of the injured and hateful child

that lives within each such man and each such woman.

MIRRORED

(For a wonderful old woman in Bristol, England)

She took my name

for the first time,

with a short, admonishing laughter of recognition.

And, suddenly

My motherless face

Lit up with relief,

Optimism, and belonging.

AT THE DAY'S END

Syllables of measured abandon,

Grace,

and silence of sharing.

This was the haiku of our mutuality.

LIKE LAND

Ever present.

Porous, and more.

Full of minerals and ore,

in its core.

Absorbing the rain of seeds.

Returning a harvest of hope.

TWO CATS

Shy, seemingly self-absorbed,

soft spoken,

Yet seductive, vigilant, even searching

We find each other.

Walk in the night's house together

And there,

I allow myself to be devoured

bit by bit, piece by piece

And

I allow myself to eat a cat

alive, bloody, and wet.

DIFFICULT COLORS

Yellow: neighborhood gossip.

Green: other's envy.

White: my failing body.

Red: your hot temper.

Blue: the distance between us.

Black: Our lonely nights.

THE SECOND POEM

Undoing

the psychic truth.

(Or, speaking from a second room

within the self?)

Something destructively large-hearted

Took him by his hand,

led him to the balcony of forgiveness.

Again and again.

THE ROOM WITHIN

Empty?

Or, just quiet?

Awaiting the arrival of the next guest?

Or, relieved by the recent departure of one?

Mute?

Or, listening to the self?

The room is alone

Or, is it?